The Magic Dust
A Fairy Tale from Ireland

Der Zauberstaub
Ein Märchen aus Irland

Berlin, 27.041.2022

Liebe Hannelore,

zu Deinem Geburtstag
die allerherzlichsten Glückwünsche
– und man ist nie zu jung
für Märchen!?

Hanne

Antic Ham – Illustration

Hans-Henner Becker – Text

The Magic Dust
A Fairy Tale from Ireland

Der Zauberstaub
Ein Märchen aus Irland

English – Deutsch

Impressum

Bibliografische Information der Deutschen Nationalbibliothek:
Die Deutsche Nationalbibliothek verzeichnet diese Publikation in der Deutschen Nationalbibliografie; detaillierte bibliografische Daten sind im Internet über http://dnb.dnb.de abrufbar.

© 2021 Hans-Henner Becker (Text), Antic Ham (Illustration)

Lektorat: Beatrice Bachnick, Mary Fullam, Michael O´Connor

Herstellung und Verlag: BoD – Books on Demand, Norderstedt

ISBN: 978-3-7534 -6469 -5

The Magic Dust

A long time ago, in County Mayo, in the far west of Ireland, a girl called Moira grew up in an old house on the great lake Conn. Her father, Eoghan, was a fisherman and her mother Fiona looked after the garden and the cattle. Her sister Cara and her brother Aenghus often took her to the weekly market in Crossmolina where they sold fruit, vegetable, and fish.

Moira always looked forward to the market. Not only were there all kinds of things to buy, but there were also jugglers displaying their skills and tricks and the old people telling stories from long ago. Moira especially liked an old woman who sold small bunches of dried flowers. And when children came, she told stories from the time before people lived in Ireland and about the fairies who still lived in little grass mounds. You were not allowed to step on these mounds because otherwise you would spend the whole day looking for the front door key, which the fairies, annoyed at being disturbed, kept hidden somewhere. Cara and Aenghus always teased and made fun of Moira because she really did believe that the fairy world existed. One day at the market when they'd finished selling their produce early, they went to fetch Moira who, as usual, was sitting listening spellbound to the old lady.

'Come on," said her brother, 'you've heard these stories a hundred times!'

'You're too old now to believe in such nonsense – old world, fairies, ghosts....!' Cara added.

'I just need to hear the end!!!' pleaded Moira.

'All right ... we'll wait for you ... as always ...,' replied Aenghus.

They then rode on a cart back to their house by the lake. The cart was pulled by the bad-tempered and cranky donkey Breck and Aenghus and Cara continued to tease Moira and laugh at her as they went along:

'You'd probably rather be with your dwarves and fairies instead of helping us with the stall at the market!' said Cara. And Aenghus, putting on a fearful scowl, said '... Puh ... imagine if there were horrible, evil, huge monsters actually living in this forest!!! And here we are, passing it through all the time!! Ho ho!!" then in gentler tone, he continued, 'Oh, Moira, no one has ever seen your fairies and dwarves. Kids' stuff! And the stupid little grassy mounds that we're not allowed to step on because of you … anyway … I'm going to get rid of them anyway when we get back!'

Moira just stopped listening and fell asleep. She knew that they would stop at the bend in the stream that flowed into Lough Conn they would top for a rest. And so they did. Moira opened her eyes.

Either Cara or Aenghus had probably put her in the moss when she´d fallen asleep. Yes, it was her old resting place – but where were Aenghus and Cara? She got up and walked the short distance to the stream where they usually brought Breck the donkey to drink. They had to be there. But when Moira got there, there was no sign of the cart, the donkey Breck, Aenghus or Cara.

'Cara, Aenghus ... where are you?!' she called out loudly.

Then she looked around and was a little surprised:

The leaves on the trees were a little bigger and greener than before, but in return the trees were only half as big as normal, and the murmur of the stream sounded a little louder. Again, she called out, this time with fear in her voice: 'Cara, Angus …?'

But no one answered her. Suddenly she heard footsteps, no, it was more like a fast patter … and as well, there was a squeaky voice giving out nonstop:

'Why didn't that stupid blackbird wake me up today! I made a point of telling her yesterday. I'll never be on time to cut the grass if that's the case. Everything always goes wrong for me … You can't rely on anyone around here. It's a mess. And then Eimear with her stupid singing yesterday. It went on for half the night! How is a fellow supposed to sleep during that…?!' Then a little figure stood in front of Moira. 'Ooooops!' he exclaimed, running away in fright, and fleeing up a tree. 'Who, … what are you?' he called out to her.

And Moira was, of course, equally surprised. Up in the tree sat a strange little fellow in a green jacket, baggy trousers and a peculiar green headgear that only very remotely resembled a hat, and which kept slipping down over his eyes.

'I am Moira from the lake farm! Fiona and Eoghan are my parents … and you … who are you?' asked Moira.

'Fiona, Eoghan, never heard of them! Who am I? What a funny question….!' he continued to rant.

All of a sudden, this strange little fellow in front of her reminded Moira of a picture the old lady at the market had shown her once before and she recalled that the lady spoke about the picture in soft, low whispers - as if she were sharing a great secret, so Moira said:

'Oh ... now I know... I think you must be a Leprechaun?!'

'What else am I supposed to be! Of course, I'm a leprechaun! And I belong to the most famous family of all leprechauns in the world!' he said boastfully.

'All right, all right,' Moira tried to calm him down, 'and please get down out of that tree! And what's your name?'

'Stupid question: My name is Callum. Everyone knows that ... hm... You don't look that dangerous ... but maybe … you bite …?'

'Whaaaaat ?!' exclaimed Moira.

'Well ... I just want to know ...!' mumbled Callum. And with that, he climbed down from his tree. 'And what are you actually doing here and why are you shouting like that? Just to disturb the peace of the fifth season here!'

'But – there are only four seasons!' said Moira pointedly.

'Ahhh … we´ve a clever one here, I think … What did I do to deserve all this? … As if I'm not punished enough with my neighbour. By the way – a lake farm, whatever that is – doesn't exist here! You'll have to come up with something better!' grumbled Callum.

'You really haven´t a clue, have you! ... Who is your neighbour then?' asked Moira.

'Her name is Eimear, and she is a Sióg, I told you, didn't I? She sings or runs around all day ... That's where her name EIMEAR comes from, it means The Quick One ... pfffff ..!' making a quick motion with his hand.

Moira didn´t understand a word, asking: 'What is a sióg? And what does your name mean?'

You know nothing either, do you!' Callum ranted. 'A sióg is a fairy and Callum – that means Pigeon,' to which Moira laughed out loud because Callum reminded her of anything but a pigeon. 'Stop laughing at me like that! My name is just Pigeon - but pigeons just don't look like pigeons - like me!'

Moira looked at him again, puzzled: 'Tell me, Pigeon ... eh … Callum, how do you get to Lough Conn from here?'

'I don't know, there's no lake named Lough Conn. Maybe you mean the lake over there,' and pointed to the right.

'Can you take me there, please?' Moira asked.

'Ah, special requests, too! But ... it's all no use anyway ... too late to do anything now … even to cut the grass ... Come on so ...!' Callum replied.

Soon they reached the lake. Moira recognized it immediately – only the water was not black as she knew it, but almost crystal clear. And she should have been able to see the lake farm from there. But there were only a few of those strange little trees with the big leaves.

'What happened? It's Lough Conn, but everything else is so different!' Moira bursted out surprised.

'What's supposed to be different here? It´s always looked like this! What are you talking about! Strange people here!!!' Callum grumbled.

Before Moira could reply, she heard a fine, beautifully soft, and enchanting melody.

'Oh no, not that again! Is there no peace around here?!' exclaimed Callum.

Then suddenly a beautiful figure stood in front of them, whose white skin seemed almost transparent and the fine face with light blue eyes was framed by jet black hair. She wore a simple dark blue dress. She was small, only about a head taller than Moira.

'Are you an elf? ' asked Moira looking surprised. 'No, no, I am the fairy Eimear,' she replied, 'Elves are tall and blond and live on an island called Iceland. Sometimes they let themselves be carried by the north-western winds and fly silently over the fields in late summer to visit us.' And then looking at Moira, she said: ' What a nice guest you've brought, Callum! '

'No way, she's not a guest! The little funny creature was standing in front of me! She fled up a tree in fear of me and I had to persuade her to come down, polite and friendly as I am, … like a pigeon!' Callum said pretentiously.

'Ok, ok, I believe you, Callum…! replied Eimear, smiling, and raising her eyebrows, then turning to Moira, 'Now sit down with us first and tell us your story! '

'Oh no … You never get any peace around here!!!' shouted Callum, but then his curiosity got the better of him.

Moira told them about the old woman and her stories, about her own family, about the weekly market and how everyone always makes fun of her and that Aenghus wants to level the grassy hills in front of the lake farm – and how she woke up and met Callum in this new place. Then she pondered for a moment and asked a little anxiously: 'But … how would I get back home from here to my family!?'

Eimear thought for a moment and said:

'You know – on a tiny island in the lake there is an ancient blue door, standing alone. Without a wall or a house. No one – not even the eldest fairies know what the door is for or who built it. But there is an old story of a fairy who walked through this door. When she came back, she told me about a country that looked almost like the one you just described. I've been to this little island a few times. The door is there, you can circle around it, but you can't open it. And what I also heard is that we fairies, dwarves and others were also supposed to have come through that door once.'

'What are dwarves?!' asked Callum looking annoyed at that. 'And you, what are you?' pointing at Moira.

'I am a human!' answered Moira.

'Ah … and probably,' Callum continued, 'those little fairies mistook you for your lovely brother who wants to flatten the little fairies' pretty grass huts and that's why they sent you here, so you can't do any harm there!'

Moira's mind was elsewhere. Then she said:

'The old woman at our weekly market once told me that there is a magic dust that forms into a key when you stand in front of the right door…! And that it's the door between the two worlds. Maybe that's the door in the lake you told me about?'

Eimear looked at her intently, asking: 'And did the old woman also know where to find the magic dust?'

'Yes. On an eagle island!' answered Moira.

'Great, ... eagle island ..., ' Callum grumbled, 'they squat on every island around here – those the good-for-nothing eagles ... we have such a plague of eagles here!!!'

'Yes,' Moira added, 'but the old woman also said that the island is shaped like an eagle.'

'There is such an island, Achaill, far in the west – off the great sea!' recalled Eimear.

'Well,' said Callum, ' ... that's right. My uncle Pink Flamingo used to tell me there was an island like that.'

'Did he look like you?' asked Moira with a grin.

'What's that supposed to mean now!!!?!! Such cheek!!!' shouted Callum.

And Eimear laughed like tinkling glass, then she considered:

'Perhaps the old woman guessed what might happen to you and gave you some advice to take with you! '

'That means I have to go to Achaill to get the magic dust to open the door to get back to my family?' Moira asked.

'I don't know, we'll have to wait and see,' said Eimear, 'but it's definitely worth a try! You know what – we'll all go there together.'

Then she looked at Callum, who immediately jumped around, startled:

'No, no, no – no way. We must go past the great mountain Nephin, with its evil mist ghosts, against which even the strongest fairies have no chance! And then that mean dragon on the Corraun Peninsula.

Chased my great uncle "Grey Heron" down to Mullaranny. Do what you like - but without me!'

Eimear, in a gentle but amused voice: 'But Callum – you´re not going to leave two helpless creatures like us defenseless at the mercy of evil forces, are you?! You, the great strong hero, around whom so many legends exist!'

Flattered, Callum replied, '... well ... so ..., it's already my job to protect you and drive the enemies up into the trees from where they tremble in fear and beg me for mercy!'

'All's well then! Tomorrow we leave!' and to Moira she whispered. 'He cannot possibly be left here alone. There'll be a disaster if we do....!'

Then Moira made herself comfortable in the large fairy mound of Eimear and immediately fell fast asleep.

The next morning the three of them set off. Callum immediately led the way, but in the wrong direction, until Eimear asked him to stop.

'You'd better go at the end – in case the enemy comes from behind!' Eimear said. Then turned and led them in the opposite direction.

'Very good idea... better safe than sorry!' muttered Callum, following them.

Eimear was very thoughtful.

'Isn't there anything the mists are afraid of?!' asked Moira.

'Well – I've heard they're extremely afraid of water!' replied Eimear.

'Great idea, going after evil spirits with a watering can ... Oh dear...,' whined Callum.

Then Eimear suddenly became very quiet, absorbed.

'I know that trick!' whispered Callum to Moira. 'She always claims afterwards that when she sits around so silently she's had contact with the others. Such rubbish! It's all mumbo jumbo!'

Then Eimear raised her head and opened her eyes saying:
'My sisters just told me that there is a stream above Beltra Lake.
So – if you dam up the stream at the narrowest point between the two hills, it will slowly create a lake ... We would then just have to run along the side where there are no mist spirits, then they can't catch us.'

Then she built a small model out of stones and earth, showing Mount Nephin and the valley ahead. When it was finished, she said: 'This should do it. Only here,' and she pointed to a spot, 'it gets very narrow! That will be difficult!' Then turning to Callum, she asked:
'Callum - you could ask your great family with all the wonderful bird names if they could help build the dam?'

'Sure - I can do that - but it will cost you! This is all sooo stressful!' he replied.

Callum disappeared, came back after some hours.

'Ok! ' he declared. 'They´ll do it. However, they want four barrels of the very finest fairy wine in return!'

Smiling, Eimear raised three fingers of her left hand.

'I warned them that you would negotiate. Typical fairies ... but ... all right ... they want to help you ...!' said Callum.

His relatives set to work, and Moira, Eimear and Callum watched as the narrow stream slowly widened and eventually swelled into a small lake. Then they set off. This time Callum voluntarily refrained from leading the way! Of course, he was not afraid, the great hero …! Soon the first mist ghosts appeared. They were great billowing mists that tried to cast an icy finger of mist across the lake, making wide arcs over the water.

'If you get into this fog … it's over … end of! … Over!' said Callum with a big dramatic gesture.

The three of them saw the billowing of the mists quicken.

'They realize they can't reach us. And you see - they never get near the surface of the water,' said Eimear.

Then they reached the spot Eimear had shown Moira and Callum on the model. And they saw the cold mists hit the water and ice the path in front of them.

Callum was getting distressed: 'Told you it wouldn't work - but nobody listens to me. How on earth are we going to get past that narrow place by the lake you showed us before?'

And Eimear was also at a loss.

'I think I know how it could work!' said Moira suddenly. 'We'll swim!'

Callum was so excited and jumped from one foot to the other, shouting:

'Yeah - great, great idea. Why didn't I think of that myself? We will just swim to the evil ghosts, splash them wet - and they'll run away in fright!'

'No, Callum!' Moira shook her head. ' You don't understand. We will only swim to the middle of the lake, they can't catch us there because they are so afraid of the water! Look again – can't you see how wide the arc is over the lake?'

Eimear let out her tinkling laugh saying: 'What a great idea. That's the way to do it. Yes, their great fear is that they will turn to water and so disappear!'

Immediately Eimear and Moira got into the lake. But Callum remained undecided on the shore.

'Oh ... no ... I completely forgot,' said Eimear, 'He can't swim! But ... !'

And so they built a small raft, put Callum on top of it – and with Eimear flying above and Moira swimming beside it, they pushed the raft along in front of them to the middle of the lake.

The mists raged above them and Callum with clenched fists, busied himself hurtling angry abuse at them. Eimear looked at Moira as they swam and rolled her eyes up to the sky. Later they arrived safely on the other side, where the mists could no longer reach them.

'Well ...! Did you see how those craven mists trembled in fear of me!' Callum said proudly.

'You are and always will be our great once-in-a-lifetime hero,' purred Eimear as she tickled his long beard.

Undisturbed, the path led them along the coast until they spotted the peninsula of Corraun from afar. There the next adventure awaited them - the mean dragon. As they walked, Callum said: 'I'm wondering how we're going to get past that big fat dragon. The stupid creature is always asking questions and according to what I´ve heard no one can answer his questions, so nobody gets through! Mean cranky beast!'

'And why does he do that?' asked Moira.

'I'll tell you – just out of boredom. Sits outside his cave all day annoying everyone!' explained Callum.

The village of Mullaranny, of which Callum had spoken before, lies off the Corraun Peninsula and is where his relatives live. The names of his uncles and aunts, however, were not those of birds, as in Callum´s village, but were called Cat, Tiger, Lion, Cheetah, Lynx and so on. When the three told them that they were leaving for Achaill the next day and would have to pass the dragon on the way, there was great whining and moaning.

'How is it that the cat people from Mullaranny are always whining?! We of the bird family are quite different!' remarked Callum snootily. But on the way to the Corraun Peninsula, he started moaning himself now too: 'Completely pointless the whole thing ... no one has ever achieved it ... they have all been eaten ... why am I here? ... we´ve no chance!'

Then suddenly the earth shook a little and there was a tremendous stench in the air. As they went around the next bend, they suddenly saw him in front of them. And in a thunderous voice the dragon said: 'Arrrgh … Well, that's a funny gang. Probably come from that lousy village with all the scaredy-cats? Are you called Wildcat or Lion's Roar or something like that?'

Callum gathered all his courage: 'They call me Callum!'

The dragon said pensively: 'Ok... Ok... the great hero Callum ... Callum ... isn't that a pigeon?! … Ooohhh, I'm shaking with fear, a pigeon, help, a pigeon!!! … And we have a fairy here, well, pfff.' Then he looked at Moira out of his red eyes and asked her: '... and who or what are you?! '

'My name is Moira, I'm human and live at the lakeside farm at Lough Conn!' answered Moira self-confidently.

'Ah! Very Interesting. Never heard of it. And what do you want? Come to visit me? How lovely!!!!' the dragon replied and started to shake with laughter.

'We want to pass you and to go to Achaill.' Moira said.

'Ok ... ok ... they want to pass meeeeee, the mighty dragon,' he shouted loud, 'hmmmm … we´ll see about that. Well, well, it's not that easy ... You'll have to solve a riddle first. Let me think!!!' There was a long pause, then, he asked: 'Mr. 'Pigeon, tell me ... What is a ... hhhmmm ... a … wheelbarrow?'

'I knew it,' muttered Callum to the other two, 'no one can answer his questions!' Then aloud: 'Well, Dragon, ... a wheelbarrow is ... something that makes everyday life … but also Sundays ... easier .... eh ... especially during the summer holidays ... '

'Ohhhh, I see … we have a real wheelbarrow expert with us!' said the dragon with an evil grin. Then he looked at Eimear: 'And you fairy, do you perhaps know it?'

Eimear has absolutely no idea what a wheelbarrow was, but she was too embarrassed to admit that to the dragon, so she just shook her head and looked away.

'How easy do my questions have to be for at least one of you to be able to answer them. It's been like this now for centuries! But we still have this little lady from the farm, on some so-called Lough Conn – Can you answer my simple question?' the dragon roared threateningly.

Of course, Moira knew what a wheelbarrow was. They had several of them on their farm, and she replied with a smile: 'Well, dragon, that's really a pretty simple question – a wheelbarrow has a wheel at the front, a box in the middle and two handles at the back. It makes it easy to move heavy or big things that you can't otherwise carry.'

For a moment there was silence. Then the dragon roared angrily, stomped, and emitted such a torrent of foul smells that the three of them felt sick. He was flailing and jumping around in circles, but eventually he disappeared into his cave, howling and cursing.

'If you had only given me a moment longer, I would have told him that too!' remarked Callum indignant.

'Isn't Callum wonderful! He knows so much!' whispered Eimear to Moira and they both giggled. Callum looked offended at them.

From the Corraun Peninsula they ferried together on a raft to the island of Achaill. There they soon met an old fairy to whom they told their plan.

'Yes, I was the guardian of the magic dust for a long time,' said the fairy in a sad voice and she pointed to one of the three island´s mountains, 'there, at the top of Slievemore, the great mountain, I lived in a deep, deep cave next to the summit. The magic dust you talked about is hidden there. Then a pair of enormous eagles nested nearby and in the end they drove me away. And the worst thing was: I didn't get to save the jar with the precious magic dust. And now I have been waiting so long for them to move on - but the eagles stayed!'

'I'm telling you, there are eagles flying all over the place in this area! But nobody listens to me!' grumbled Callum. 'Have you got a tin pot and a wooden spoon? I'm going to make some real noise and scare those cowardly scrawny birds away!'

'I wonder if that will help?' Moira thought doubtfully.

Then the three of them set off on the strenuous path to the summit. On their way, glorious sunshine was followed by rain and storm. Suddenly right in front of them sat a massive eagle. When Callum, at a safe distance, began to bang furiously on the pot, the eagle just raised and turned its head a little and tilted it at an angle, as if to say, 'That's a welcome change. But what's that funny little green fellow doing there?' Apart from this he doesn't stir.

'What are we going to do now?' asked Moira in despair.

But Eimear sang one of her fairy songs again and slowly the eagle lowered its head and gently fell asleep. Moira and Eimear looked warningly at Callum. He better not say anything about the song – and above all – he better not wake the eagle. And Moira and Eimear tiptoed into the dark cave. Callum, the great hero, did not go in, saying he had to 'keep watch' outside. In the cave there were unfamiliar and strange noises, like a kind of laughter or hissing. Everything got louder and louder and more eerie the closer they got to the farthest, deepest corner of the cave. Then – there it was!! They could see it!! The jar was tucked away in a small nook, so they grabbed it quickly and left the gloomy cave, accompanied by a strange murmuring sound. Back outside, they wanted to make their way back immediately, but then Callum clumsily dropped the tin pot! There was a loud clatter as the pot rolled all the way down the hill. The three stood frozen, looking fearfully at the eagle.

The eagle opened its eyes slowly and suspiciously. Then it shook its head and straightened up. Eimear had no time to sing her song again.

And so the huge eagle swooped down on the three of them. Eimear, Moira, and Callum took off running. Eimear let out a desperate cry.

And a moment later, a dense fog rose from the sea at the foot of Slievemore.

'We must reach the fog' shouted Eimear to the others, 'run as fast as you can!'

'But aren't they the dangerous mist ghosts again?' asked Moira.

'No, no these were sent by the fairies of the sea. They are helping us!' replied Eimear breathlessly. Moira could hear the eagle's wing flapping behind her and tightened her grip on the jar. Then Eimear remembered an old trick of the fairies. She took the shadows of herself, Moira and Callum and cast them behind her, forward and to the sides. This greatly confused the eagle, who now no longer knew where the three of them actually were. Only a few meters separated them from the dense fog, and Callum felt the eagle strike at him with its sharp claws ... and rip his green hat from his head.

But then the three of them disappeared into the fog and the eagle flew off in a rage – still holding Callum's hat in its enormous claw.

They rested on the beach of the village of Dugort, also called the Silver Strand.

'That was a close one!!!' gasped Moira.

'I've had enough of such adventures for now!' replied Callum. 'Although … without me, none of this would have worked! But the first thing I need is a new hat!'

Eimear and Moira laughed heartily. Then Eimear stood at the sea's edge and looked out over the waves, thanking the fairies of the sea who had sent them the thick mist.

The way back was much easier. They passed the cave, from which she could still hear the wailing and clamour of the dragon.

'They all whine a lot here in this place ...!' thought Moira grinning.

They rested in Mullaranny and continued their journey the next day. Because the dammed lake at Mount Nephin had grown even larger, they passed the misty spirits raging with fury on the other side without difficulties.

Back at Lake Conn, they rowed a small boat to the island where the solitary door stood. Moira and Eimear both tried to open the door one after the other, but the magic dust did not turn into a key. Then Callum had an idea: 'Maybe you two need to touch the jar together at the same time, a fairy and a human!'

So they did. And really – the magic dust turned at once into a key. The door swung open, and they saw a deep light.

'If you hadn´t had me!!!' said Callum cockily, growing a little taller.

'Will you come with me ... to my side?!' Moira asked them both excitedly.

Eimear looked at Moira thoughtfully and then she answered:

'Oh, you know, I'd rather live here with my fairy sisters - and, as you know by now, someone has to look after Callum all the time. It's better here than with you.' Of course, Callum was not at all amused at what Eimear said and gave her one of his usual disgruntled looks. Eimear ignored him and continued talking to Moira: 'But you must tell the children there on the other side about the land here. Maybe the old storyteller was here once as a child too, and maybe someday there will be another child, who believes in the old stories and will visit us here! And of course, Moira, you will always be welcome here!'

Callum nodded in agreement with Eimear, but he looked a little sad because Moira was leaving. Then he added excitedly: 'But we will visit you, too!'

The three hugged each other and then Moira stepped into the light that came from the doorway…

The next moment she was lying again on the moss in the clearing in the forest. She heard the shouts of Cara and Aenghus: 'Moira ... Moira ... Hellooooo, where are you???!!!'

Then suddenly they stood in front of her.

'Where have you been? We've been looking for you for hours!' they asked her excited.

On the way back to the lake farm Moira told them about her adventure, about Eimear, Callum, the mist spirits, the dragon, the eagle, the fairy, the magic dust, and the key. Needless to say, the two didn´t believe a word Moira said, but to Moira´s delight, the old storyteller at the market believed every single word Moira told her about her wonderous adventures!

Later on, Moira built tiny fences around the little mounds in front of the lake farm so that no one would step on them and disturb her beloved fairies. And sometimes she went back to that magical spot next to the river in the woods to visit her friends Eimear and Callum in Fairyland.

Der Zauberstaub

Vor langer Zeit wuchs in der Grafschaft Mayo ganz im Westen von Irland in einem alten Haus an dem großen See ´Conn` das Mädchen Moira auf. Ihr Vater Eoghan war Fischer und ihre Mutter Fiona kümmerte sich um den Garten und das Vieh.

Ihre große Schwester Cara und ihr Bruder Aenghus nahmen Moira oft zum Wochenmarkt nach Crossmolina mit, auf denen sie Obst, Gemüse und Fisch verkauften. Moira freute sich immer sehr auf den Wochenmarkt. Es gab dort nicht nur allesmögliche zu kaufen, sondern es zeigten auch Gaukler ihre Kunst und die Alten erzählten Geschichten aus längst vergangener Zeit. Moira mochte besonders eine alte Frau, die kleine Sträuße aus getrockneten Blumen anbot. Wenn Kinder kamen, erzählte sie von der Zeit, bevor die Menschen in Irland lebten. Sie erzählte von Feen, die in kleinen Grashügeln lebten. Auf diese Hügel durfte man nicht treten, weil man sonst den ganzen Tag den Haustürschlüssel suchen würde, den die Feen, ärgerlich über die Störung, irgendwo versteckt hielten. Cara und Aenghus machten sich immer wieder über Moira lustig, die natürlich ganz fest an all das glaubte.

Einmal, an einem der Markttage – sie hatten alles, was sie mitgebracht hatten, schnell verkauft – holten sie Moira wieder bei der alten Frau ab, der Moira gebannt zuhörte.

„Nun komm schon", sagte ihr Bruder, „die Geschichten hast Du doch schon hundertmal gehört!"

Und Cara: „Du bist doch nun schon zu alt, um an solchen Unsinn zu glauben – alte Welt, Feen, Geister …!"

„Ich muss nur noch das Ende der Geschichte hören!!!", rief Moira aufgeregt.

„Ist ja gut … wir warten auf Dich … wie immer …", antwortete Aenghus.

Der Karren, auf dem sie zurückfuhren, wurde von dem meist schlecht gelaunten und bockigen Esel Breck gezogen. Und natürlich lachten die beiden großen Geschwister Moira weiter aus.

„… Du wärst wohl am liebsten bei deinen ´Zwergen und Feen`, anstatt uns auf dem Markt zu helfen!" neckte sie Cara.

Und Aenghus, der eine fürchterliche Fratzen zog, sagte: „Puh … stellt Euch vor, in diesem Wald, durch den wir fahren, leben schreckliche, böse, riesige Ungeheuer … huuuuh!" Dann etwas sanfter: „Ach Moira, niemand hat Deine Feen und Zwerge je gesehen. Kinderkram! Und die blöden kleinen Grashügel, auf die wir Deinetwegen nicht treten dürfen, werde ich auch erst einmal wegschaufeln, wenn wir zurück sind!"

Später hörte Moira den beiden einfach nicht mehr zu und schlief ein. Sie wusste, irgendwann an der Biegung des Baches, der in den See Conn floss, würden sie Rast machen – wie immer. Und so war es.

Ihre Geschwister hatten sie wohl in das Moos gelegt, nachdem sie eingeschlafen war. Moira schlug die Augen auf. Ja, es war ihr alter Rastplatz – doch wo waren Aenghus und Cara? Sie stand auf und ging zu dem Bach, an dem sie den Breck normalerweise tränkten. Dort mussten sie ja sein. Doch als Moira dort ankam, war nichts von dem Karren, dem Esel, Aenghus oder Cara zu sehen.

„Cara, Aenghus … wo seid Ihr?!" rief sie ganz laut.

Dann schaute sie sich etwas überrascht um: Die Blätter der Bäume waren etwas größer und grüner als sonst, dafür waren die Bäume aber nur halb so groß und das Rauschen des Baches hörte sich ein wenig lauter an. Wieder rief sie, diesmal mit Angst in der Stimme:

„Cara, … Aenghus …?!"

Doch niemand antwortete ihr. Plötzlich hörte sie Schritte, nein, es war eher ein Trippeln. Dazu schimpfte eine piepsige Stimme ununterbrochen:

„Warum hat mich die blöde Drossel heute nicht geweckt! Ich hatte es ihr doch gestern ausdrücklich gesagt. So komme ich nie pünktlich zum Schneiden der Gräser. Alles läuft immer schief. Auf niemanden kann man sich hier verlassen. Ein einziges Chaos. Und dann noch Eimear mit ihrem dusseligen Gesang gestern. Die halbe Nacht ging das! Wer soll denn dabei einschlafen … !"

Dann stand jemand plötzlich vor Moira.

„HUCH!", rief ein komischer kleiner Kerl aus, rannte vor Schreck los und flüchtete auf einen Baum.

„Wer, … was bist Du denn?", rief er ihr von oben zu.

Moira war natürlich ebenso überrascht. Auf dem Baum saß ein Männchen in einer grünen Jacke, ausgebeulten Hosen und einer eigenartigen grünen Kopfbedeckung, die nur ganz entfernt an einen Hut erinnerte, und die ihm immer wieder über die Augen rutschte.

„Ich bin Moira vom Seebauernhof. Fiona und Eoghan sind meine Eltern. Und Du … wer, was bist Du?", fragte ihn Moira.

„Ogottogottogott … noch so ein vorlautes Wesen …? Fiona, Eoghan, nie gehört! Ich, was soll ich schon sein!" schimpfte er weiter.

Irgendwie erinnerte der komische kleine Kerl Moira an ein Bild, das ihr die alte Frau auf dem Wochenmarkt einmal gezeigt und ihr etwas zugeflüstert hatte, als ob sie ihr ein sehr großes Geheimnis verriet.

„Ahhh … jetzt weiß ich es!", rief Moira. „Du bist ein Leprechaun?!"

„Was soll ich denn sonst sein! Natürlich! Und ich gehöre zur berühmtesten Familie aller Leprechauns!", und er streckte sich dabei so in die Höhe, dass er zuhause bei Moira gerade über die Tischkante hätte schauen können.

„Ist ja gut", versuchte Moira ihn zu beruhigen, „ … komm endlich runter von dem Baum! … und sag, wie heißt Du denn?"

„Blöde Frage, Callum heiße ich. Mich kennt doch jeder … hm … gefährlich siehst Du ja nicht aus … oder beißt Du etwa?"

„Waaas soll ich tun?!"

„Naja … fragen darf man ja wohl…", und dabei kletterte Callum tatsächlich herunter. „Und was machst Du hier eigentlich und warum schreist Du so herum und störst hier einfach die Ruhe der fünften Jahreszeit?"

„Es gibt aber doch nur vier Jahreszeiten!", meinte Moira.

„Ahhh … auch noch besonders schlau, die junge Dame!", grummelte Callum weiter. „Womit habe ich das alles verdient, als ob ich mit meiner Nachbarin nicht genug gestraft bin. Übrigens – einen ´Seebauernhof´, was immer das ist – gibt es hier nicht! Da musst Du Dir schon etwas Besseres einfallen lassen!"

„Du hast ja keine Ahnung!', rief Moira und fragte ihn: „Wer ist denn Deine Nachbarin?"

„Sie heißt Eimear und ist eine Sióg, sagte ich doch schon, oder? Sie singt den ganzen Tag oder rennt herum. Daher auch ihr Name: EIMEAR, das bedeutet ´die Schnelle´ …pfffff…!", und Callum machte eine schnelle Bewegung mit der Hand.

Moira verstand kein Wort, fragte: „Was ist eine Sióg? Und was bedeutet Dein Name?"

„Du weißt auch gar nichts! Eine Sióg ist eine Fee und ich bin Callum – das bedeutet die … `Taube´." Moira lachte laut auf, weil Callum an alles Mögliche erinnerte, nur nicht an eine Taube. „Lach nicht so blöde. Mein Name ist halt ´Taube´ – aber Tauben sehen halt nicht so aus wie Tauben – also wie ich!"

Moira schaute ihn wieder verständnislos an, fragte weiter: "Sag einmal, Tau… eh Callum, wie kommt man hier zum See ´Conn´?"

„Kenn ich nicht, aber dahinten ist ein See, vielleicht meinst Du den?", und Callum zeigte nach rechts.

„Kannst Du mich hinführen?", fragt ihn Moira.

„Ah … auch noch Sonderwünsche! Aber … hat ja alles sowieso keinen Zweck … alles zu spät heute … zum Gräserschneiden sowieso … also, dann komm schon…!", und Callum ging mit ihr fort.

Bald erreichten sie den See. Moira erkannte ihn sofort wieder – nur war das Wasser nicht schwarz, wie sie es kannte, sondern fast glasklar. Und eigentlich hätte sie von dort aus den Seebauernhof sehen müssen. Aber dort waren nur ein paar dieser eigenartigen kleinen Bäume mit den großen Blättern.

„Was ist passiert?", fragte Moira, „Das ist doch mein See, aber ansonsten ist irgendwie alles anders!"

„Was soll hier anders sein? Sieht immer so aus, der See! Was redest Du da eigentlich?! Hier gibt es komische Leute!!!", schimpfte Callum. Bevor Moira antworten konnte, hörten sie eine feine, zauberhafte Melodie.

„Oh nein! Nicht schon wieder!!", rief Callum. „Hat man hier nie seine Ruhe?"

Vor ihnen stand ein wundervolles Wesen. Die weiße Haut schien fast durchsichtig und das feine Gesicht mit hellblauen Augen war von tiefschwarzem Haar umrahmt. Sie war klein, vielleicht etwas größer als Moira und trug ein einfaches dunkelblaues Kleid. „Bist Du etwa eine Elfe?", fragte Moira. „Nein, nein … ich bin die Fee ´Eimear´. Elfen sind groß und blond und wohnen auf einer Insel, die Island heißt. Manchmal lassen sie sich vom Wind zu uns treiben und fliegen dann lautlos im Spätsommer über die Felder, um uns zu besuchen. Was für einen netten Gast hast Du mitgebracht, Callum?!"

„ … Nix da, … von wegen … ein Gast! Stand plötzlich vor mir, die Kleine! Sie flüchtete aus Angst vor mir auf einen Baum und ich musste sie erst überzeugen herunterzukommen, höflich und freundlich, wie ich bin, … wie eine Taube halt!", erzählte Callum.

„Ich ahne es, Callum…!", antwortete Eimear lächelnd und zog die Augenbrauen leicht nach oben und zu Moira gewandt: „Nun setz Dich erst einmal zu uns und erzähl uns, was passiert ist!"

„Auch das noch …!!!", schimpfte Callum – aber dann siegte seine Neugier.

Und Moira erzählte von der alten Frau, ihren Geschichten, von ihren Eltern und Geschwistern, von dem Wochenmarkt, dass sich alle immer über sie lustig machen und dass Aenghus die Grashügel vor dem Seebauernhof einebnen will. Dann überlegte sie einen Moment und fragte etwas ängstlich: "Wie komme ich eigentlich zurück nach Hause?"

Eimear dachte lange nach und sagte dann:
„Weißt Du – auf einer winzigen Insel im See steht eine uralte blaue Tür. Einfach so. Ohne Mauer oder Haus. Niemand – auch nicht die ältesten Feen wissen, was die dort soll und wer sie gebaut hat. Es gibt aber eine Geschichte von einer Fee, die einst durch diese Tür geschritten ist. Als sie zurückkam, erzählte sie von einem Land, das fast so aussah, wie Du es gerade beschrieben hast. Ich war schon ein paar Mal auf dieser kleinen Insel. Die Tür steht dort, man kann sie umkreisen, aber nicht öffnen. Und was ich hörte: Auch wir Feen, Leprechauns oder Zwerge sollen einmal durch diese Tür gekommen sein. Nur die sehr kleinen Feen sind wohl nicht mitgekommen."

„Was sind Zwerge?!", fragte Callum und schaute dabei verärgert, „und Du, was bist Du eigentlich?", und zeigte auf Moira.

„Ich? … Ein Mensch bin ich!", antwortet Moira.

„Nie gehört, ´Mensch´!", grummelte Callum weiter. „Wahrscheinlich haben diese kleinen Feen Dich mit Deinem ´netten´ Bruder verwechselt, der die hübschen Grashäuschen der kleinen Feen platt machen will und Dich deswegen hierhergeschickt, damit Du keinen Schaden anrichten kannst!"

Moira war aber mit ihren Gedanken ganz woanders:
„Die alte Frau auf unserem Wochenmarkt erzählte einmal, dass es einen Zauberstaub gibt, der sich zu einem Schlüssel formt, wenn man vor der Tür steht, die die Welt der Menschen mit der der Feen und Zwerge verbindet. Vielleicht ist das die Tür, von der Du erzählt hast?"

Eimear schaute sie aufmerksam an, fragte: „Und wusste die alte Frau auch, wo der Staub zu finden ist?"

„Ja! Auf einer Adlerinsel!", antwortete Moira aufgeregt.

„Toll, Adlerinsel…", murmelte Callum „... auf jeder Insel hocken sie hier, diese nichtsnutzigen Adler … wir haben hier eine wahre Adlerplage!!!"

„Ja", fuhr Moira fort, „aber die alte Frau meinte auch, dass diese Insel wie ein Adler geformt sei."

„Es gibt so eine Insel. Achaill, ganz im Westen – vor dem großen Meer!", erinnerte sich Eimear.

„Nun ja", sagte Callum, „stimmt ... hat mein Onkel ´Rosa Flamingo´ auch immer erzählt, dass es so eine Insel geben soll."

„Sah er so aus wie Du?", fragte Moira grinsend.

„Was soll das jetzt wieder heißen?!?!?! Unverschämtheit!!!", schimpfte Callum.

Eimear lachte und es klang, als ob ein Vorhang aus Glas sich bewegt, dann überlegte sie laut: „Vielleicht ahnte die alte Frau, was Dir passieren könnte, und gab Dir einen Rat mit!"

„Das heißt", fragte Moira, „ich muss nach Achaill, um den Zauberstaub zu holen, mit dem ich die Türe öffnen kann, damit ich wieder zu meinen Eltern und Geschwistern gelange?"

„Vielleicht … ich weiß nicht", sagte Eimear, „aber einen Versuch ist es wert! Weißt Du – wir drei gehen dort gemeinsam hin", dann blickte sie Callum an.

Dieser hüpfte sofort aufgeschreckt herum und schimpfte: „Nein, nein, nein – auf gar keinen Fall. Da müssen wir am großen Berg Nephin vorbei … mit seinen bösen Nebelgeistern, gegen die selbst die stärksten Feen keine Chance haben! Und dann dieser gemeine Drachen auf der Corraun-Halbinsel. Hat einmal meinen Großonkel ´Grauer Reiher´ runter bis nach Mullaranny gejagt. Macht was ihr wollt – aber ohne mich!"

„Aber Callum", sagte Eimear belustigt, „Du willst doch uns zwei hilflose Wesen nicht schutzlos den bösen Geistern ausliefern. Du großer starker Held, um den sich so viele Sagen ranken."

Geschmeichelt antwortete Callum: „Nun ja … also … eigentlich ist es schon meine Aufgabe, Euch zu beschützen und die Feinde auf die Bäume zu treiben, wo sie vor Angst zittern, mich um Gnade anflehen!"

„Dann ist ja alles gut! Morgen brechen wird auf!" Zu Moira flüsterte Eimear: „Ihn kann man unmöglich hier allein zurücklassen. Das gibt sonst eine Katastrophe …!"

Dann machte Moira es sich in dem Feenhügel von Eimear gemütlich und schlief sofort tief und fest ein.

Am nächsten Morgen machten die drei sich auf den Weg. Callum ging sofort voran, aber in die falsche Richtung, bis ihn Eimear bat anzuhalten.

„Du gehst besser am Ende – falls sie von hinten kommen!" Und sie führte dann die beiden in die entgegengesetzte Richtung…

„Sehr gute Idee… sicher ist sicher!", murmelte Callum und folgte ihnen.

„Sagt einmal, gibt es denn eigentlich gar nichts, vor dem die Nebel Angst haben?!", fragte Moira die beiden anderen.

„Nun – ich habe gehört, dass sie extrem wasserscheu sind!", antwortete Eimear.

„Wie? Was? Wollt Ihr etwa die bösen Nebelgeister nass spritzen – mit einer Gießkanne, … oder was?!", jammerte Callum. „Und überhaupt - wie kommen wir bloß an ihnen vorbei?"

Eimear wurde ganz still und nachdenklich.

„Ich kenne das!", flüsterte Callum Moira zu. „Sie behauptet danach immer, dass sie, wenn sie so stumm rumsitzt, ´Kontakt zu den anderen´ hat. Blödsinn! Alles Hokuspokus!"

Eimear hob den Kopf und öffnete die Augen.

"Meine Schwestern haben mir gerade erzählt, dass es einen Bach oberhalb des Beltra-Sees gibt. Also - wenn man den Bach an der schmalsten Stelle zwischen den beiden Hügeln aufstaut, dann entsteht langsam ein See. Wir müssten dann nur an der Seite entlanglaufen, wo es keine Nebelgeister gibt, dann können sie uns nicht erwischen."

Dann baute sie ein kleines Modell aus Steinen und Erde, das den Berg Nephin und das vor ihm liegende Tal zeigte. Als es fertig war, sagte sie: "So müsste es gehen. Nur hier", und sie zeigte auf eine Stelle, "wird es sehr, sehr eng! Das wird schwierig!"

Dann wandte sie sich an Callum und sagte: "Callum, kannst Du Deine große Familie mit all den wunderbaren Vogelnamen fragen, ob sie beim Bau des Damms helfen könnten?"

„Klar – kann ich machen – aber das wird teuer für Dich! Ein Stress ist das hier alles!!", sagte Callum und ging los.

Nach einiger Zeit kam er zurück.

„Also – ok, sie machen es!", verkündete Callum. „Allerdings - sie wollen dafür vier Fässer vom allerfeinsten Feenwein haben…!"

Lächelnd hob Eimear drei Finger ihrer linken Hand.

„Ich habe sie gewarnt, dass Du handeln wirst. Typisch Feen … aber … na gut … sie wollen uns ja auch helfen …!"

Callums Verwandte machten sich ans Werk und Moira, Eimear und Callum beobachteten, wie der schmale Bach langsam breiter wurde und schließlich zu einem kleinen See anschwoll. Dann machten sie sich auf den Weg. Diesmal verzichtete Callum freiwillig darauf, voranzugehen. Und natürlich hatte er keine Angst, der große Held ..!

Schon bald zeigten sich die ersten Nebelgeister. Es waren große wabernde Nebel, die versuchten einen eiskalte Nebelfinger über den See zu werfen, wobei sie immer einen großen Bogen über das Wasser machten.

„Wenn Du in diesen Nebel gerätst … dann ist es aus … Ende … Schluss!", warnte Callum und unterstrich das mit einer dramatischen Geste. Sogleich sahen die drei, wie das Wabern der Nebel schneller wurde.

„Sie erkennen, dass sie uns nicht erreichen … und siehst Du – sie kommen nie in die Nähe der Wasseroberfläche!", rief Eimear aus.

Dann erreichten sie die enge Stelle und sahen, wie die kalten Nebel über das Wasser schlugen und den Weg vor ihnen vereisten. Callum war verzweifelt: „Sagte ich doch,", zeterte Callum, „dass das nicht klappt – aber auf mich hört ja keiner! Wie sollen wir da bloß vorbeikommen?!"

Und auch Eimear war ratlos.

„Ich glaube, ich weiß, wie es funktionieren könnte", verkündete Moira plötzlich, „wir schwimmen!"

Callum sprang von einem Bein auf das andere und jammerte: „Ja – klasse, tolle Idee. Warum bin ich nicht selbst darauf gekommen? Wir schwimmen einfach zu den Geistern, spritzen sie nass – und die rennen dann vor Schreck weg …!"

„Nein, Callum", sagte Moira und schüttelte den Kopf, „Du verstehst mich nicht. Wir schwimmen in die Mitte des Sees und dann weiter bis zum anderen Ufer. Dort können sie uns ja nicht kriegen, weil sie so wasserscheu sind! Schau doch noch einmal, welchen großen Bogen sie immer über die Oberfläche des Wassers machen."

Eimear ließ ihr Glaslachen hören, sagte: „Was für eine großartige Idee, Moira. So machen wir es. Ja, ihre große Angst ist es, dass sie wieder zu Wasser werden und so verschwinden!"

Sogleich stiegen Eimear und Moira in den See. Callum aber blieb unschlüssig am Ufer stehen.

„Ach … nein … ich habe es ja völlig vergessen!", sagte Eimear. „Er kann doch nicht schwimmen! Aber … !"

Und dann bauten sie ein Floß, auf das sie Callum setzten, schwammen in die Mitte des Sees und schoben das Floß vor sich her.

Die Nebel tobten über ihnen und Callum ballte die Fäuste und beschimpfte sie wild. Eimear sah Moira an und rollte mit den Augen. Dann landeten sie an einer Stelle, wo die Nebel sie nicht mehr erreichen konnte.

„Na ja … es ist doch gut, dass ich mitgekommen bin! Habt Ihr gesehen, wie die Nebelgeister vor Angst vor mir zitterten?!", prahlte Callum wie immer sehr stolz auf sich.

„Du bist und bleibst unser großer, einmaliger Held", schnurrte Eimear, während sie seinen langen Bart kraulte.

Unbehelligt folgten sie dem Weg an der Küste entlang, bis sie von Weitem die Halbinsel Corraun entdeckten. Dort wartete das nächste Abenteuer auf sie – der gemeine Rätseldrache.

Während sie wanderten, maulte Callum: „Nun bin ich gespannt, wie wir jetzt an diesem dicken Drachen vorbeikommen sollen. Das blöde

Vieh stellt immer Fragen. Wie ich hörte, kann die niemand beantworten. Dann lässt er einen einfach nicht durch! Gemeiner Kerl!"

„Und warum macht er das?", fragte Moira.

„Ich sag Dir – nur aus Langeweile. Sitzt den ganzen Tag vor seiner Höhle und ärgert alle!", erklärte Callum.

Vor der Halbinsel Corraun lag das Dorf Mullaranny, von dem Callum schon erzählt hatte. Dort lebten seine Verwandten. Ihre Namen waren aber nicht die von Vögeln, wie beim ihm zuhause, sondern sie hießen Katze, Tiger, Löwe, Gepard, Luchs und so weiter und so weiter. Als die drei Callums Tanten und Onkel berichteten, dass sie am nächsten Tag nach Achaill aufbrechen wollten und dabei auch am Drachen vorbeimussten, erhob sich wieder ein großes Gejammer und Gezeter.

„Dass die Katzenleute aus Mullaranny immer jammern müssen! Wir von der Vogelfamilie sind da ganz anders!", bemerkte Callum etwas hochnäsig.

Später, auf der Corraun-Halbinsel fing er nun genau mit dieser Meckerei wieder an: „Völlig sinnlos das Ganze … hat noch nie jemand geschafft … werden alle aufgefressen … warum bin ich nur hier?"

Plötzlich bebte die Erde und ein ungeheurer Gestank lag in der Luft. Nach der nächsten Biegung sahen sie den Drachen plötzlich vor sich.

Und mit Donnerstimme sagte er: „Na, das ist ja eine lustige Truppe. Kommt wohl aus dem lausigen Dorf mit all den Angsthasen oder besser Angstkatzen? Heißt Ihr vielleicht ´Wildkatze´ oder ´Löwengebrüll´, oder so?"

„Man nennt mich Callum!", sagte er und nahm dabei all seinen Mut zusammen.

„Soso … was für ein Held … Callum … Callum … heißt das nicht Taube?! Ooohhh, ich zittere vor Angst, eine Taube, eine Taube!!! Da hätten wir hier noch eine Fee, nun ja, pfff … !", und dann schaute Moira mit seinen dunklen, roten Augen an, „… und wer oder was bist Du denn?!"

„Ich heiße Moira, bin ein Mensch und komme vom Seebauernhof am See Conn!", antworte Moira.

„Aha. Interessant. Nie davon gehört. Und was wollt Ihr? Mich besuchen? Wie nett von Euch!!!!", und der Drache fing an, sich vor Lachen zu schütteln.

„Wir wollen an Dir vorbei und nach Achaill", antwortet Moira.

„Soso, Ihr wollt also an miiirrrr vorbei und nach Achaill. Interessant. Nun, nun, das geht aber nicht so einfach … zunächst müsst Ihr ein Rätsel lösen. Lasst mich überlegen …" Nach einer langen Pause sprach er weiter, „Herr Taube, sagen Sie mal … was ist eigentlich eine … hhhmmm … ´Schubkarre´?!"

„Ich wusste es", flüsterte Callum zu den beiden anderen, „seine Fragen kann niemand beantworten!". Dann laut: „Also, Drache, … eine Schubkarre ist … wenn man so will … etwas, was den Alltag aber auch die Sonntage … einfacher macht … eh …, besonders in den Ferien …"

„Ohoooo, … da haben wir ja einen richtigen Schubkarrenexperten!", polterte der Drache böse grinsend. „Und Du Fee, weißt Du es vielleicht?"

Eimear schüttelte nur den Kopf. ´Was soll das sein, eine ´Schubkarre?!´, dachte sie.

„Wie einfach müssen denn meine Fragen sein, damit wenigstens jemand von Euch sie beantworten kann. Seit Jahrhunderten geht das so! Nun, dann hätten wir noch diese kleine Lady von diesem Bauernhof … an diesem See Conn!

Kannst Du denn meine einfache Frage beantworten?", brüllte der Drache gefährlich.

Aber Moira wusste natürlich, was eine Schubkarre ist.

Sie hatten mehrere davon auf ihrem Hof und antwortete: „Also, Drache, das ist wirklich eine ziemlich einfache Frage – eine Schubkarre hat vorn ein Rad, in der Mitte eine Kiste und hinten zwei Griffe. Damit kann man schwere oder große Sachen einfach bewegen, die man sonst nicht tragen kann."

Einen Moment war es ganz still. Dann brüllte der Drache wütend, trampelte und sonderte einen Schwall übler Gerüche ab, dass es den Dreien schlecht wurde. Schließlich jagte er dreimal um sich herum und verschwand heulend und keifend in seiner Höhle.

„Hätte er mir nur einen Moment länger Zeit gelassen, hätte ich ihm das auch gesagt!", bemerkte Callum.

„Ist Callum nicht wundervoll! Er weiß so viel!", flüsterte Eimaer zu Moira und beide kicherten.

Von der Corraun-Halbinsel setzten sie dann mit einem Floß zur Insel Achaill über. Dort trafen sie bald eine Fee, der sie von ihrem Plan berichteten.

Die Fee erzählte traurig: „Ja, ich war lange die Hüterin des Zauberstaubes", und zeigte auf einen der drei Berge der Insel, „und dort, ganz oben auf dem Slieve More, dem großen Berg, lebte ich in einer tiefen Felsspalte nahe dem Gipfel, die in eine Höhle führte. Dort ist auch der Zauberstaub verborgen. Dann nistete ganz in der Nähe ein gewaltiges Adlerpaar, das mich schließlich vertrieben hat. Und das Schlimmste ist: Ich kam nicht mehr dazu, das Kästchen mit dem wertvollen Zauberstaub aus der Höhle zu retten. Und nun warte ich schon so lange, dass sie weiterziehen – aber sie blieben und sind immer noch da …"

„Sag ich doch, dass in der Gegend überall die Adler rumfliegen! Aber auf mich hört ja niemand!", schimpfte Callum wieder einmal und fragte die Fee: „Hast Du einen Topf und einen Holzlöffel? Ich werde mal richtig Lärm machen und diese feigen Vögelchen verscheuchen!"

´Ob das hilft?´, dachte Moira nachdenklich.

Schließlich machten sich die drei auf den anstrengenden Weg zum Gipfel. Immer wieder änderte sich das Wetter: Auf herrlichen Sonnenschein folgten Regen und Sturm. Schließlich standen sie vor dem Felsen mit der Spalte. Genau davor saß ein gewaltiger Adler. Dieser schlug langsam und argwöhnisch die Augen auf. Als Callum in sicherer Entfernung begann, wie wild auf den Topf zu schlagen, hob der Adler nur ein wenig den Kopf und neigte ihn schräg, als ob er sagen wollte: ´Das ist mal eine willkommene Abwechslung. Aber was treibt dieser komische kleine grüne Kerl da?`

Aber ansonsten bewegte er sich nicht.

„Was machen wir jetzt bloß?", fragte Moira verzweifelt.

Dann sang plötzlich Eimear wieder eines ihrer Feenlieder und langsam senkte der Adler den Kopf und schlief sanft ein. Warnend schauten Moira und Eimear zu Callum: Er sollte jetzt bloß nichts dazu sagen und den Adler dadurch wieder wecken. Moira und Eimear gingen auf Zehenspitzen hinein in die dunkle Felsspalte.

Callum, der große Held, ging nicht mit, sagte, er müsse draußen ´Wache halten`. In der Höhle gab es unbekannte und eigenartige Geräusche, wie ein Lachen oder ein Rauschen.

Und das alles wurde immer lauter und unheimlicher, je mehr sie sich der tiefsten Stelle der Höhle näherten. Und da war es! Das kleine reich verzierte Kästchen! Es stand von Steinen halb verborgen in einer kleinen Nische. Schnell nahmen sie es an sich und verließen die düstere Höhle, begleitet von diesem schaurigen Raunen.

Wieder draußen wollten sie sich sofort vorsichtig auf den Rückweg machen. Doch dann ließ Callum ungeschickt den Topf fallen! Es schepperte laut, als der Topf den Berg hinunterkullerte. Wie erstarrt blieben die drei stehen, blickten ängstlich zu dem Adler, der sein Haupt aufrichtete. Eimear hatte keine Zeit ihr Lied zu singen, damit der Adler wieder einschlief. Und so stürzte sich der riesige Vogel auf die drei. Eimear, Moira und Callum rannten los. Eimear stieß einen verzweifelten Schrei aus. Einen Augenblick später stieg vom Fuße des Großen Berges vom Meer dichter Nebel auf.

„Wir müssen den Nebel erreichen!!!", rief Eimear den anderen zu, „Lauft, lauft so schnell ihr könnt!"

„Sind das nicht die gefährlichen Nebelgeister?", rief Moira.

„Nein, nein, … den haben die Feen des Meeres geschickt. Sie wollen uns helfen!", antwortete Eimear atemlos.

Moira hörte hinter sich schon die Flügelschläge des Adlers. Da entsann sich Eimear einer alten List der Feen. Sie nahm die Schatten von Moira, Callum und von sich, warf sie nach vorn, nach hinten und zu den Seiten. Das verwirrte den Adler so sehr, dass er jetzt nicht mehr wusste, wo die drei nun eigentlich waren. Nur noch wenige Meter trennten sie von dem rettenden dichten Nebel, da spürte Callum wie der Adler mit seinen scharfen Krallen nach ihm schlug … und seinen grünen Hut vom Kopf riss.

Dann aber verschwanden die drei im Nebel und der Adler flog wütend davon – immer noch Callums Hut in der gewaltigen Kralle.

Am Strand des Dorfes Dugort, der auch silberner Strand genannt wird, ruhten sie sich aus.

„Puh … das war aber knapp!!!", keuchte Moira.

„Ich habe erst einmal genug von solchen Abenteuern!", antwortete Callum, „… obwohl … ohne mich hätte das ja alles nicht geklappt! Aber das Allererste, was ich brauche, ist ein neuer Hut!!!"

Eimear und Moira lachten. Dann stand Eimear am Meeressaum und blickte hinaus auf die Wellen und dankte den Feen der See, die ihnen den dichten Nebel gesendet hatten.

Der Rückweg war viel einfacher. Sie kamen an der Höhle vorbei, aus der sie immer noch das Grummeln des Drachen hörten. In Mulranny machten sie Rast und am nächsten Tag setzten sie ihre Reise fort. Weil der aufgestaute See am Berg Nephin noch größer geworden war, kamen sie ohne Schwierigkeiten an den Nebelgeistern vorbei, die auf der anderen Seite vor Wut tobten.

Am See Conn angekommen, ruderten sie mit einem kleinen Boot zu der Insel, auf der die Tür stand.

Moira und Eimear versuchten nacheinander die Tür zu öffnen, jedoch der Zauberstaub verwandelte sich nicht einen Schlüssel. Dann hatte ausgerechnet Callum eine Idee: „Vielleicht müsst Ihr beide das Kästchen gleichzeitig und zusammen berühren, eine Fee und ein Mensch!"

Das taten sie dann auch. Und wirklich – der Zauberstaub verwandelt sich in einen Schlüssel. Moira steckte ihn in das Schloss, die Tür ging auf und sie sahen ein geheimnisvolles Licht.

„Wenn Ihr mich nicht hättet!!!", grinste Callum selbstbewusst und wurde wieder ein wenig größer.

„Kommt Ihr mit … zu mir?!", fragte Moira die beiden aufgeregt.

Eimear zögerte einen Moment, schaute Moira an und sagte dann nachdenklich: „Ach weißt Du, ich möchte lieber bei meinen Feenschwestern bleiben – und, Du weißt es ja inzwischen, irgendjemand muss ja ständig auf Callum aufpassen. Das geht hier besser als bei Euch."

Callum schaute Eimear verständnislos und wie immer ein wenig verärgert an.

„Aber", fuhr Eimear fort, „Du musst den Kindern dort auf der anderen Seite von dem Land hier berichten. Vielleicht ist die alte Geschichtenerzählerin früher einmal als Kind auch hier gewesen und vielleicht gibt es ja irgendwann wieder ein Kind, das an die alten Geschichten glaubt und uns hier besucht. Und Du bist natürlich immer bei uns willkommen!"

Dabei nickte Callum, der etwas traurig schaute, weil Moira fortging.

„Und wir besuchen Dich auch!!!", ergänzte er aufgeregt.

Dann umarmten sich die drei noch einmal herzlich und Moira trat ein in das Licht, das aus der Türöffnung schien.

Im nächsten Moment lag sie wieder im Moos und hörte die Rufe von Cara und Aenghus: „Moira … halloooooo!!!".

Dann standen sie vor ihr: „Wo warst Du denn die ganze Zeit? Wir suchen Dich seit Stunden!"

Auf dem Rückweg zum Seebauernhof erzählte Moira von ihrem Abenteuer, von Eimear, von Callum und seinen Verwandten, den Nebelgeistern, dem Drachen, der anderen Fee, dem Adler, und natürlich von dem Zauberstaub. Natürlich glaubten die beiden Moira kein Wort – wohl aber die alte Geschichtenerzählerin, der Moira am folgenden Markttag atemlos von ihrem großen Abenteuer berichtete.

Moira baute kleine Zäune um die kleinen Grashügel vor dem Seebauernhof, damit niemand mehr auf sie trat und die Feen darin störte. Und manchmal ging sie zurück an die Stelle am Bach im Wald – und besuchte Eimear und Callum im Feenland.

Karte der abenteuerlichen Reise von
Moira, Eimear und Callum

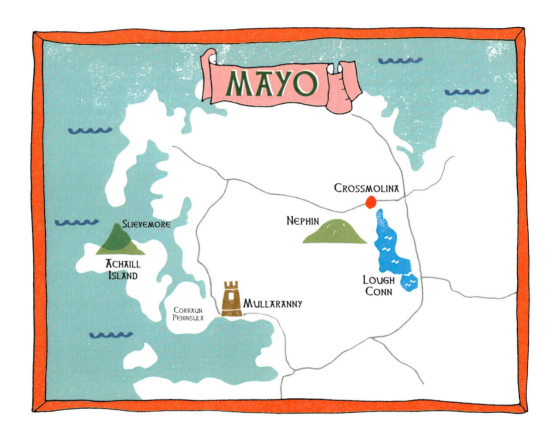

Map of the adventurous journey of
Moira, Eimear und Callum

ANTIC-HAM – Illustration

Antic-Ham (born in Seoul, South Korea) is based on Achill, Mayo, Ireland since 2006. Together with Francis Van Maele she runs the art print production, REDFOXPRESS. She creates artist books using various techniques such as screen printing, collage, illustration, and photography and participates frequently to book fairs and exhibition in many countries, collaborating with artists and writers from all over the world.

Antic-Ham (geboren in Seoul, Südkorea) lebt seit 2006 mit Francis Van Maele auf Achill im Westen Irlands und führt dort mit ihm den Kunstbuchverlag REDFOXPRESS. Sie gestaltet Kunstbücher mit Techniken wie Siebdruck, Collage, Illustration und Fotografie. Ham ist mit ihren Werken auf Buchmessen und Ausstellungen in vielen Ländern vertreten und arbeitet mit Künstler- und SchriftstellerInnen auf der ganzen Welt zusammen.

www.anticham.de

HANS-HENNER BECKER – Text

Hans-Henner Becker (geboren in Düsseldorf, Deutschland), lebt in Berlin. Er ist Autor von Theaterstücken und Gedichten, organisiert seit Jahren irische Festivals in Berlin und vermittelt Musikerinnen und Musiker. Seit über 40 Jahren fährt er regelmäßig nach Irland, ist der irischen Literatur und Musik tief verbunden. Und die Insel Achill ist nun seine zweite Heimat geworden.

Hans-Henner Becker (born in Düsseldorf, Germany), lives in Berlin. He is author of plays and poems, organises Irish festivals in Berlin for year and works as a music agent. He has been travelling frequently to Ireland for over 40 years, deeply attached to Irish literature and music. And the island of Achill has become his second home.

www.hanshennerbecker.de

…. und/and …

Beatrice Bachnick, Mary Fullam, Francis Maele und Michael O'Connor:

Euch ganz herzlichen Dank für die Durchsicht, die Hilfe bei der Übersetzung, die Geduld und die vielen hilfreichen Hinweise!

Thank you so much for your review, translation help, patience, and many helpful comments!